the art POSTER MAKING

by John Smith

ISBN 1 871517 20 6

Osmiroid Creative Leisure Series

About the Author

John Smith studied at Cardiff College of Art, taking his NDD in Book Illustration and Lettercutting. Following an obligatory two years in the RAEC in Germany, he taught pottery in Cardiff and was later responsible for the Art Department at the Pontypool College of Further Education. He returned to Germany for nine years, and was Head of Art at King's School with the British Families Education Service. He then returned to the UK to lecture at the Mary Ward College of Education in Nottingham. He now lives in King's Lynn and lectures at the Norfolk College of Arts and Technology.

He is a lecturer demonstrator for the Osmiroid Pen Company and frequently exhibits with the prestigious Society of Scribes and Illuminators. He inscribed the lists of Bishops and Deans for Llandaff Cathedral and the Victoria Cross Vellum for the Cathedral's Welch Regiment Chapel.

He has work published in "British Bookplates" (David and Charles), both volumes of "Modern Scribes and Lettering Artists" (Studio Vista/Trefoil), "Sixty Alphabets" (Thames and Hudson), "Florilege" (Alain Mazeran, Paris), The Calligrapher's Project Book (Collins) and Osmiroid's "Making Calligraphy Work for You".

The Osmiroid Poster Making Kit provides everything you need to start creating exciting posters. As your interest and skill in the art of poster making grows, you may wish to purchase other materials to develop some of the further ideas outlined in this book as well as your own particular interests.

CONTENTS

Poster designed for King's Lynn Town Guides.

Programme cover using lettering as a background texture.

INTRODUCTION

This book is about making posters, but it is about a lot more besides. What, after all, is a "notice" if it is not a "poster"? And what is a "showcard" if it not a "notice"? Menus, book-jackets, record-sleeves, place names, announcements, logos and the like are all closely allied to the poster. They share the same fertile common ground of lettering and design and contribute, separately or collectively to that vast area of written or printed ephemera – the communicative arts.

For obvious reasons this book includes a large section on lettering. This is a necessity. Some of us enjoy an almost subliminal delight in the forms which make up our alphabet and would happily meditate with Ben Shahn on his "Love and Joy about Letters". And there can be very few indeed who have not, in adolescence, made self-conscious, if not secretive attempts to improve their signatures, at least.

The ability of the potential poster-maker varies from the trained artist, perhaps lavishly equipped and accommodated, to those who insist that they cannot draw a straight line (which is quite difficult anyway!). Somewhere between are those like the club secretary, (coerced), who not only have to work on a shoe string but on the kitchen table as well. Others may be anchored in nostalgia for a past filled with images of letters topped with snow! For all these, this book is intended. It offers guidance, a source of interest, and a way forward.

A final word of encouragement. Some people are born poster designers; some achieve great posters; but most of us have posters "thrust upon us". If you belong in this latter category, accept the challenge. It need not be a daunting task, and you don't *have* to draw a single letter. There's scissors in the drawer and a multitude of headline letters in those old magazines. The wallpaper left over from the dining room will make a good background. Let's go!

Television title designed for BBC.

Poster/invitation for SSI Anniversary Dinner.

ALISON URWICK

DIAMOND·JUBILEE·DINNER·OF·THE·
SOCIETY·OF·SCRIBES·&·ILLUMINATORS·

MENU·WILL·BE·SERVED·IF·A·WRITTEN·REQUEST·IS·SENT·WITH·TICKET·

A·VEGETARIAN

Tuesday 12th May, 1981, from 6·30 to 10·30 p.m.
The Royal Over-Seas League, Over-Seas House,
Park Place, St. James's Street, London S.W.1.
Tickets £8 each. Applications for tickets for
members & friends must be received by March 1st.

APPLICATIONS·

· EVENING · DRESS· OPTIONAL ··· 1921·SSI·1981··· 1921·SSI·1981··· 1921···1981

MATERIALS AND EQUIPMENT

The materials needed to make a poster are those that are easily available to you and those with which you like working best! This statement should dispense with the long list of items that artists endeavour to collect within an arm's length of their drawing board. People work differently and we are all quick to discover what suits us best. I rarely use a lay-out pad — an item frequently described as vital, and I once catapulted a constellation of blots across a nice piece of work, following the advice of a scribe who recommended using a rubber band to secure a paper guard to my drawing board. It may not have been bad advice but it didn't work for me! The following are mentioned, therefore, with these provisos in mind, and comprise only a few of the important tools of the trade. Later chapters will identify others and explain their use.

Drawing Board and T-Square The Osmiroid wooden Drawing Board is perfectly adequate, suppliers of office equipment can also offer a range of plastic substitutes which hold the paper while the accompanying set square operates from ready marked measurements on the board.

Papers This will depend on your choice of media. Sugar paper may be ideal for collage but it will not suit pen and ink. If your poster is to be reproduced you will generally want to work in black on white. For "one-off" posters avoid the weak pastel shades and sometimes try using white or light colours on a dark background. Tracing paper is useful if you are contemplating any formal work.

Pencils The average pencil is an HB (Hard/Black), H to 6H gets increasingly hard; B to 6B increasingly soft.

Erasers Buy the best. Cheaper ones will shroud your work in a grey mist.

Square-Edged Pens Osmiroid calligraphy pens, sets and Dip Nib sets are ideal as they offer a range of interchangeable nibs. All Osmiroid Dip Nib pens are fitted with an ink reservoir.

"Automatic Pens" are useful for extra large calligraphic work. The five pronged "music" pen and the "shadow" pen are included in this range.

Brushes Buy what you can afford and look after them! Square-edged nylon brushes are excellent for large work and are not expensive.

Inks and Colours These should be water based. Bottled ink is convenient but not as good as chinese stick-ink which you rub down with distilled water. For opaque colour, designers' gouache cannot be bettered though the less expensive poster colour is a good substitute. Splendid colour effects can also be achieved with the widely available and excellent range of felt tip pens and markers, their transparency allowing for beautiful "over-printing" effects.

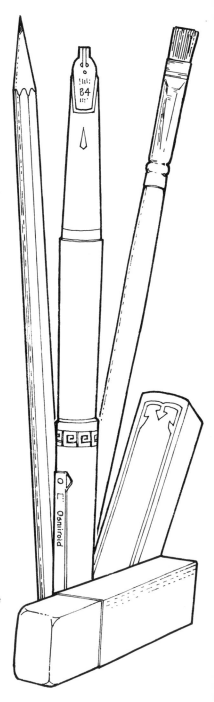

One way of attracting attention!

Playing with letter-shapes.

Poster from a photograph and collage.

About Posters . . .

The design of any poster will differ from the design of any other. That, at least, is the theory, and for the dedicated student it is no bad precept to follow. Treat each one as a new ''problem'' and it will show in the originality and quality of your ''solution''. One or two general rules apply, however, and although they are matters of common sense they are listed below as reminders.

1. Your poster must attract attention. Assume that most passers-by have the attention span of a cuckoo in a Swiss clock, then you'll know what you're up against.
2. Make it easy to read.
3. Keep it brief.
4. ''Say'' the essentials boldly.
5. Suit your style of lettering to your theme.
6. Don't forget anything important. Omit the date of your Whist Drive and you'll pass your evening playing ''Patience''.

A few other hints to bear in mind.

1. Keep a scrap book of other people's ideas. This will mean collecting brochures, advertisements etc.
2. Allow your taste to drift ''up-market'' – where the best designers are usually to be found, but keep an eye on the others just in case.
3. Learn to look and to criticise. Ask yourself where the efforts of others have gone wrong.
4. Use whatever you admire shamelessly in your work; it will acquire something of your own in the process.

. . . and their Production

Your way of working will depend on four principal factors

1. The time you have available.
2. The materials you have on hand.
3. How your poster will be reproduced.
4. Your ability.

Enjoyment is one of the keys to success in creative work, and if you are happy doing it, it will show in the quality of the results. So become enthusiastic when things are going well, it may encourage you to take a few worthwhile risks.

If time presses, think ahead, plan accordingly and contrive any short cuts you can devise. Start with a large piece of paper and trim it down later.

Keep your scissors to hand. It can help you cut corners – metaphorically.

Use photo-copying facilities to advance your design quickly. If you are engaged on a short-run production, colour parts of each by hand. You can vary your colour schemes this way, and have fun doing so.

Remember that we are all, as designers, "on the road to Damascus". Your skills may be in their infancy but this book sets out to help you over a few of the obstacles along the way. The author is still trying to get over one or two himself!

LETTERING

The Skeleton Alphabet

It is understandable that newcomers to the craft of lettering are attracted to alphabets beyond that which is illustrated on the accompanying page. They would be well advised, however, to take more than a glance at what is known as the Skeleton Alphabet, for it is on this simple geometrical structure that other alphabets are based. Its value to the lettering artist should not be underestimated.

The letter form is based on a circle. Five "round" letters, C, D, G, O and Q follow this shape. Directly related, because their characters are drawn in a rectangle of similar area to this circle, are the nine letters A, H, N, T, U, V, X, Y, Z. These are known as "three-quarter" letters because their width is accommodated between two vertical margins $\frac{1}{8}$th less on either side. Except for the M and W, which are "wide" letters, all other letters are "narrow", and apart from the letter "I" are contained roughly in half a square.

Uniform Height Letters should be drawn between faint guide lines to establish uniform height but the round letters and the "points" of A, M, V and W should fractionally exceed these borders or they will look smaller, especially if they are adjacent to flat topped characters like E and Z. There is a frequent tendency for the amateur to draw letters on a single base guide line. Unless the work is of a free, informal nature, the guide line to indicate height should also be drawn. The subsequent visually satisfying band of letters play an important part in fundamental design and it is no less significant that letters are more easily recognised by their tops as will be observed in the following diagram.

window on NOTTINGHAM

If the bases only of these letters had been illustrated it would not be possible to identify the words. Revolutionary though it may seem, I have often suggested that were handwriting to be penned *below* a guide line rather than *on* a guide line, the craft of calligraphy and indeed communication would be better served.

Upper and Lower Case Capitals are often referred to as upper-case letters; small letters as lower-case. These typographic terms have been handed down by printers who took their capital type from an upper case and their small letters from a case which was lower. Sometimes they are also referred to as majuscules and minuscules.

Skeleton Alphabet, capitals.

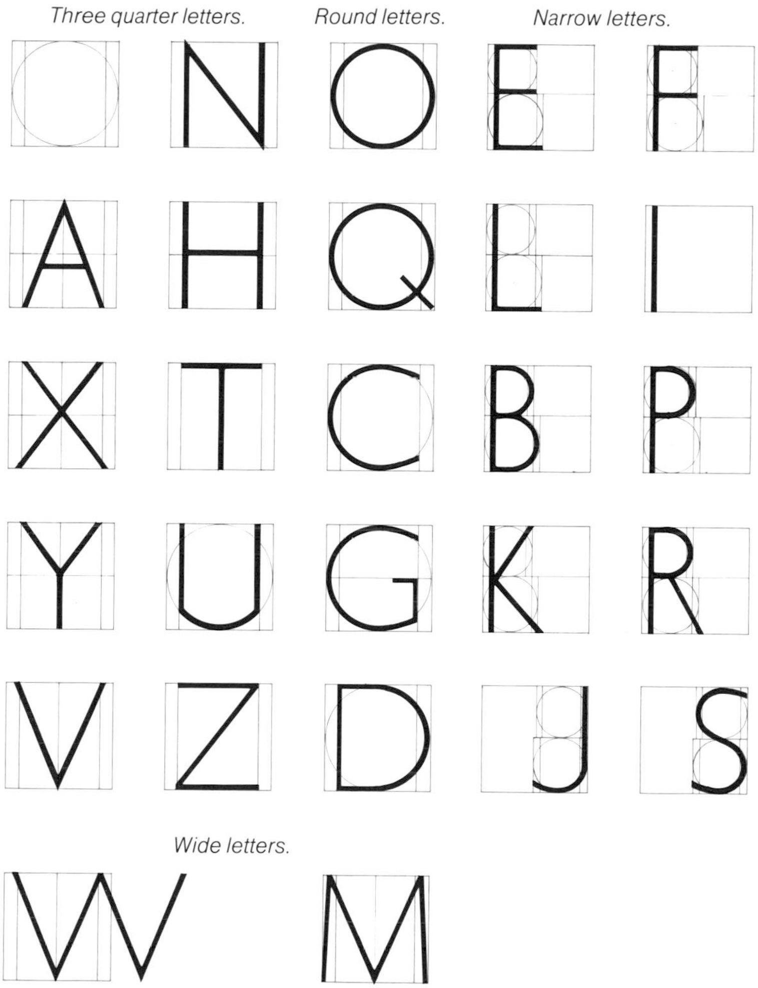

Three quarter letters.   *Round letters.*   *Narrow letters.*

N O E F

A H Q I

X T C B P

Y U G K R

V Z D J S

Wide letters.

W M

Numerals to accompany capitals or capitals with lower-case lettering.

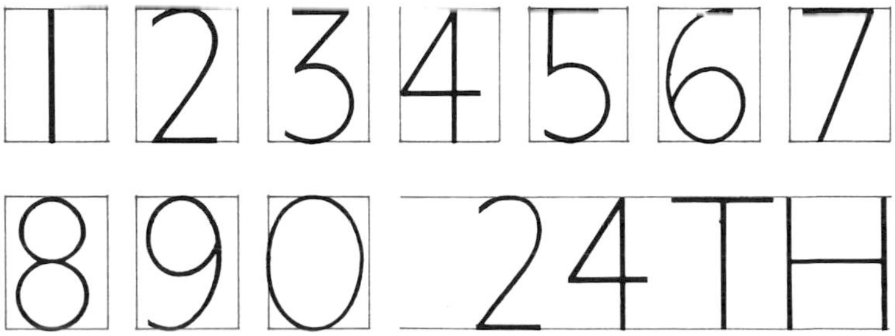

1 2 3 4 5 6 7

8 9 0 24TH

Ascenders and Descenders The rising strokes which exceed the body height and the tails which go below the base line of lower-case letters are known as ascenders and descenders respectively.

The "x" Height The height of the basic form of a lower-case letter, not including the extra length of ascenders and descenders, is called the "x" height.

Proportion of Capitals to Lower-Case Letters The body of the lower-case letter should be roughly ³/₅ths the height of its accompanying capital. Ascenders and descenders should be approximately ²/₅ths of the capital height. Making a capital letter twice the size of the "x" height is quite wrong and leads to ungainly proportion. If the recommended ratio surprises, it would be of interest to realise that the Ministry of Transport, whose lettering for traffic signs must be regarded as vital, uses a capital height just ⁴/₁₀ths higher than the body of its lower-case.

Three quarter letters. *Round letters.* *Narrow letters.*

Wide letters.

Skeleton Alphabet, lower-case letters and some alternatives.

Proportion of capital to lower-case letter.

Numerals that may be used with lower-case letters.

Numerals Since numerals will not easily relate to a geometric pattern I have drawn them within the "three-quarter" rectangle to indicate my concept of their form and proportion.

Numerals placed with capitals are drawn the same height. Numerals which accompany lower-case letters more readily match the text if even numbers are a little higher than the "x" height, and odd numbers correspondingly extend below the base line.

Making use of the Skeleton Alphabet.

ENTERTAINMENT

Squash Tournament

ADMISSION BY TICKET ONLY

Working with varying thicknesses of felt and plastic pens.

VOLUNTEERS ARE URGENTLY REQUIRED FOR THE NEXT

Tickets available from Alison Cribley or committee members

REFRESHMENTS WILL BE PROVIDED IN ROOM L 304 AFTER THE PERFORMANCE

Applications to Mr Douglas J. Goss, Head of Dept., Eastern European Studies

Lettering with a fine drawing pen.

REPRESENTATIVES IN BIRMINGHAM, CARDIFF, EXETER , HULL AND NOTTINGHAM

Using a fine nib with thinned white gouache.

BAND OF THE ROYAL SCOTS DR

Working with a small brush and white gouache.

Spacing

The first of the accompanying illustrations shows that you cannot space letters effectively by leaving the same gap between each. Since the space inside letters also has to be taken into account, judging by eye seems to be the most acceptable method. As a guide, place adjacent straight-sided letters furthest apart, rounded letters closest together and allow a compromising space between a round letter and a straight-sided one.

Another system, especially useful when using dry transfer letters, is to establish the distance between the 1st and 2nd letters, then place the 3rd in such a position that the 2nd sits comfortably between the 1st and the 3rd.

SEMINAR

Incorrect spacing.

SEMINAR

Better arrangement.

Poster produced simply by pasting down strips of information together with a Christmas card.

Party invitation: lettering within drawings can be effective.

Inter-word spaces should approximate to the letter height, a rough guide being an imaginary "o" between the words. Space between lines of writing, e.g. the supplementary wording at the bottom of a poster, will vary from job to job. Allowing little space can be attractive but where lower case letters are involved, care should be taken not to allow a clash of ascenders and descenders.

Developments from Skeleton Alphabet.

Jackdaws love my big sphinx of quartz

Swift felt-pen work.

THREE ZEBRAS CLUB

The effect of shading background around letters.

THE QUICK BROWN FOX JUMPS OVER THE LAZY DOG

About sixty cod fish eggs will make a quarter pound of very fizzy jelly

Capitals and lower-case with simple serifs.

Except mid week zippy hovercrafts jockey along beside quays

This sort of handwriting is useful for fast supplementary information.

CHILDREN'S PARTY
with Mr Abracadabra

Informal fun lettering produced with black felt pen and brush with white gouache on a medium toned background.

Eight quaint jovial zebras could wake my playful fox

More playful "invented" lettering.

17

Producing Roughs

Most designers "think" graphically. Ideas may begin in the mind but, for most of us, they come to life only when they are set down on paper. Normally, this marks the first stage in a series (which may become a saga!) of changes and modifications. So work small so that you can get lots of ideas down. Scaling-up the best of them is explained later.

Some beginners find these early stages tiresome. They are impatient to get on with the full-scale, final project. Don't be tempted! Learn to put your trust in expediency – not hope. Sort out your problems at the rough stage and you will sail through the rest easily. Well more easily, anyway!

A rough can determine the importance of the elements in your design. It can give you advance warning of problems. It can become a finished work in itself. A rough will certainly have a lively, spontaneous quality that will be difficult to re-capture later, but you will learn to do this by practice. Just don't be tempted to skip this stage, meanwhile.

Finished poster scaled-up and
developed from one of the roughs.

Writing with the Square-edged Pen

The flow of ink from pen to paper will be affected by the angle of your drawing board or working surface. Discover a comfortable angle which suits you best; it will depend on how you hold your pen and also the type of pen you are using. A fountain pen or cartridge pen requires less of a slope than a "dip" pen. Your work should be protected from the grease of your hand and a few sheets behind it will form a more resilient surface.

Osmiroid's Calligraphy and Poster Sets contain "dip" nib holders fitted with an adjustable metal reservoir. The nib should be inserted so that the tip of the reservoir is in contact with its underside. Other types of nib have separate "slip-on" reservoirs. The reservoir holds and controls the flow of ink. Contrary to expectation, you should fill a "dip" pen with a brush. Of course, it is possible to dip the pen into the ink but the resulting work will be less sharp. Clean your pen from time to time.

Sit comfortably, hold the pen with a relaxed grip and get it working on some scrap paper. You will soon discover that calligraphy's characteristic thick and thin strokes and the subtle graduations, one to another, are achieved by maintaining the square-edged nib at a constant angle. Practice pattern making and the letter-making strokes indicated. The basic underlying shape of the Round Foundational Hand is the circular "O".

The relationship of nib width to its letter height is very important and determines the "weight" of the letter. In the Round Foundational Hand the "x" height should be four times the width of the nib. Ascenders and descenders extend a further 3 nib widths above and below the "x" height "tram lines". Draw faint guide lines with a sharp pencil. At a later stage you might guess the lengths of ascenders and descenders and use only the "x" height "tram lines" as a guide.

Holding the pen at a constant 30° angle to the writing line will provide a slightly thicker vertical stroke than a horizontal stroke. A common mistake is to hold the pen at too steep an angle, resulting in heavy "arches" and "feet" and over-thin verticals, all depriving the letter of good calligraphic form. The number of strokes and "pen-lifts" varies from letter to letter. The order and direction of pen movements are not difficult to remember. As you become more experienced you will be able to make slight variations of angle and pen movements to suit your individual style.

The Osmiroid "dip" pen is available in many nib sizes.

Filling the nib with a brush.

The Round Foundational Hand illustrated is a modernised version of that developed by Edward Johnston who based his research on a 10th century manuscript.

The 30° (2 o'clock) angle.

Forming the serif.

"Lift" the edge of the nib to form the sharply pointed base of the "V" (and similar "W") the capital letter is drawn the same way.

The 2nd stroke of the "V" and parts of other letters similar to this shape (e.g. the 1st stroke of the capital "A") can be drawn by altering the pen angle on its downward movement.

MARK SMITH

Rough for examination poster.

*Exhibition piece for SSI Exhibition;
designers gouache on dark paper.*

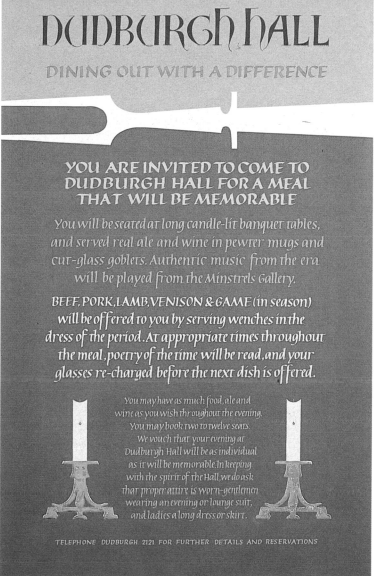

*Poster for examination: pen lettering in
designers gouache on coloured paper.*

Writing Capitals with the Square-edged Pen

The proportion of capital letters to accompany the Round Foundational Hand should emulate Roman Inscriptional Lettering, the finest example of which is to be found at the base of Trajan's Column in Rome. Reference to the Skeleton Alphabet which analyses it will also be beneficial.

Like the Round Foundational Hand, capitals are based on the circular "O" and apart from a few subtle exceptions are made with the same 30° angle to the writing line. The C, O, S, U, V, W, X and Z are similar to the lower case. The diagonal strokes contained in the letters A, M, N, U, W, X and Y are made with a pen angle of about 45° and the comparatively thin uprights of the letters M and N will have to be achieved with a pen angle as steep as 60°.

Part of "Together in Concert" poster showing work with "music" and "square edged" pen.

Roman Capitals drawn with the "square edged" pen and suitable to accompany the Round Foundational Hand.

Proportion of capital, lower-case, ascender and descender.

Working in Colour

Flower·show

The IS Shop

RECREATION

coffee morning

Spring Ball poster showing ''positive''
and ''negative'' letter shapes.

The Italic Hand

The name of this style gives a clue to its identity for it was developed during the Italian Renaissance to give a swift, elegant and rhythmic pen letter. It is characterised by its lightness in weight, its forward slope, springing arches and slightly compressed form based on an elliptical "O". It is a versatile script and is widely used and much enjoyed by present day calligraphers. It can be less formal than the accompanying personal version and may be cursive (joining as shown in the word "Theatre"). It lends itself happily to flourishes but they should not run riot!

The italic hand.

Use five pen widths for an italic "x" height. A further four pen widths give extravagant ascenders and descenders while seven pen widths account for the capital. A pen angle of 45° to the writing line is usually recommended but I choose to retain a flatter angle so that a horizontal movement will be marginally thinner than a vertical one. Simple "lead in" hooked serifs are used for informal writing. The forward slope of the letter should be consistent and any angle between about 5° and 12° is acceptable.

Menu: italic with small capitals. A formal symmetrical arrangement.

MENU
❖

Jambon de Bayonne et Manque
BAYONNE SMOKED HAM WITH FRESH MANGOES
❖

Queue de Lotte Marseilles
FILLET OF MONK FISH, FLAVOURED WITH PERNOD, WITH
TOMATOES, MUSSELS & PRAWNS
❖

Pintade Poêlé Fructidor
GUINEA FOWL IN AN ORANGE AND LEMON SAUCE
GARNISHED WITH GRAPES & ORANGE
❖

Haricots Verts au Beurre
BUTTERED FRENCH BEANS

Pommes Persilées
PARSLEY POTATOES
❖

Coeur de Laitue Caprice
HEART OF LETTUCE FILLED WITH APPLE AND CELERY
❖

Plateau des Fromages de France
SELECTION OF FRENCH CHEESES
❖

Croquembouche Avignon
A CREATION OF CHOUX-PASTRY FILLED WITH CREAM & HAZELNUTS

Flan Alsacienne
SLICES OF APPLE & KIWI FRUIT IN A FLAN

Pavlova
CREAM FILLED MERINGUE AND FRUIT
❖

Café

COFFEE

WINES : BEAUJOLAIS NOUVEAU 1985 · MACON BLANC 1983 ·

Games evening poster: photograph, using ready made materials.

Menu cover design: photocopied and coloured by hand.

Freely drawn capitals combine elegantly with collage.

Poster for Gilbert and Sullivan operetta. Drawn originally in black but printed in colour on coloured paper. (Three colours for the price of two!).

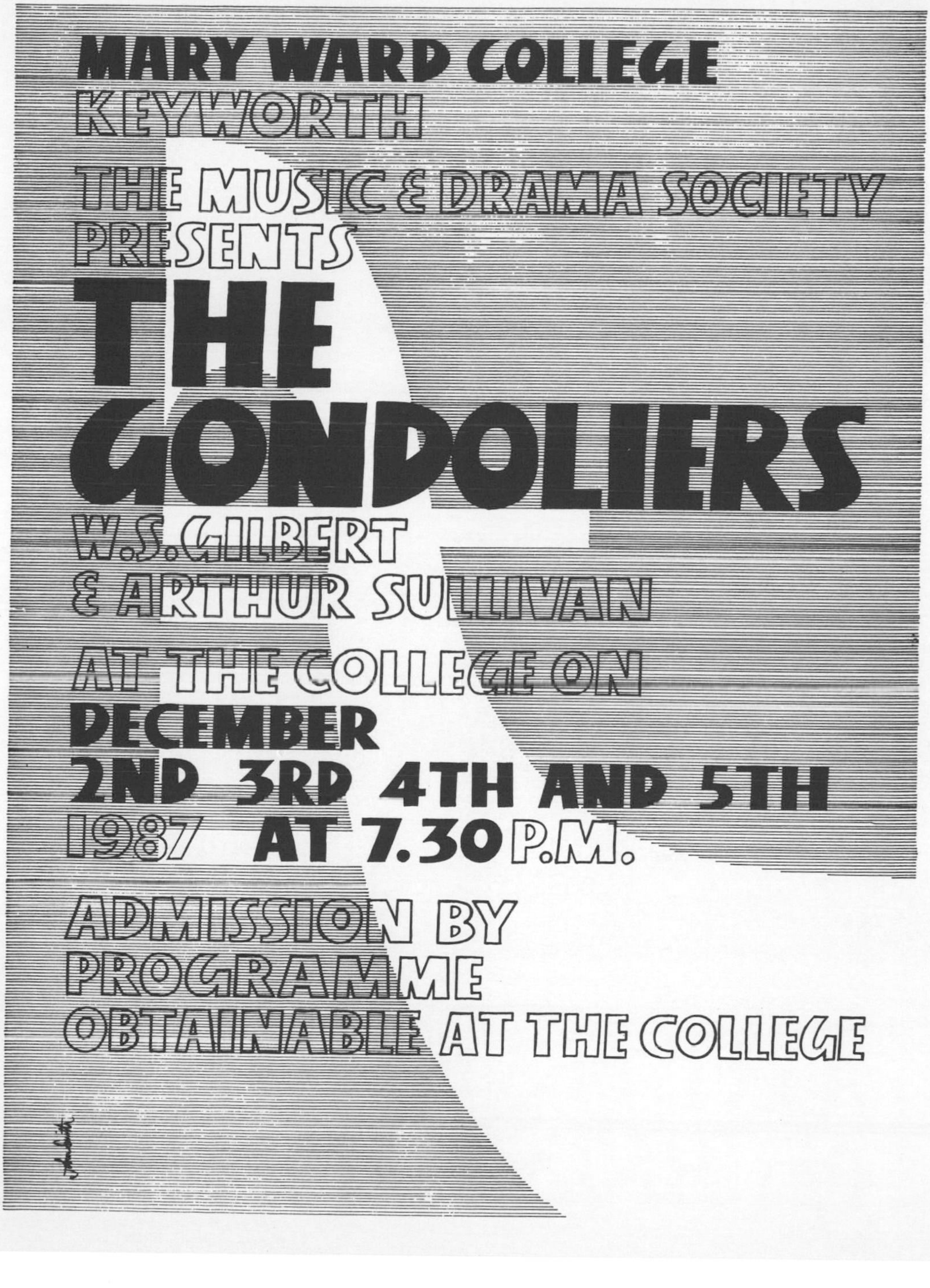

MARY WARD COLLEGE
KEYWORTH
THE MUSIC & DRAMA SOCIETY
PRESENTS
THE
GONDOLIERS
W.S. GILBERT
& ARTHUR SULLIVAN
AT THE COLLEGE ON
DECEMBER
2ND 3RD 4TH AND 5TH
1987 AT 7.30 P.M.
ADMISSION BY
PROGRAMME
OBTAINABLE AT THE COLLEGE

The Left Hander

If you are left handed, take heart — so was Leonardo da Vinci!

There are many fine calligraphers who are left handed. The illustrated notes attempt to give a basis on which the left hander might work. It is important however to discover what suits you individually; the position you hold your pen and the angle of your paper could vary considerably.

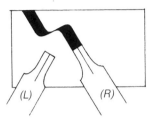

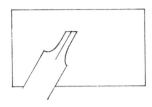

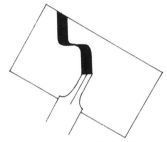

The problem confronting the left handed writer wishing to make the calligraphic movement produced by the right hander.

The solution partly solved by the use of a "left-oblique" pen.

The left hander using a left-oblique pen and, by tilting the writing paper, producing the required calligraphic stroke executed by the right hander.

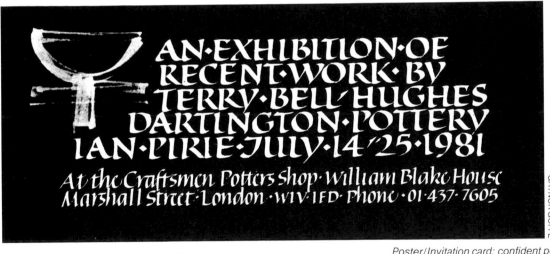

GAYNOR GOFFE

Poster/Invitation card: confident pen capitals sit comfortably with a running italic on a well arranged "page". (The art work would have been produced on black and "reversed" in the printing process).

Freely drawn pen lettering for Carol Concert programme.

Gothicised Italic

There are many variations of this type of lettering, the style of which deserves a better descriptive title. Sometimes referred to as "Pointed Italic", the hand emulates the calligraphic qualities of Italic writing and borrows some of the attraction of Gothic or "Black Letter" alphabets.

abcdefghijklmn
opqrstuvwxyz
1234567890

ABCDEFGHIJK
LMNOPQRST
UVWXYZ
1234567890

The approach is very much a personal one, diversifies as the mood takes one and lends itself to informality, flourishes and freedom.

While there is a temptation for the beginner to adopt this style it is better accomplished when confidence in the Round Hand and Italic has been gained.

Roman Capitals

The Romans raised the standard of lettering in their day to superb heights. Their alphabet represents the source from which all Western letter forms derive. Made up of simple geometric forms, thick and thin strokes and graduating curves, it has obvious influences of the "Square edge", and was probably first painted with a flat brush or reed before being incised with mallet and chisel.

The Trajan Column Inscription (AD 114).

Beautifully drawn Roman capitals by Tom Perkins.

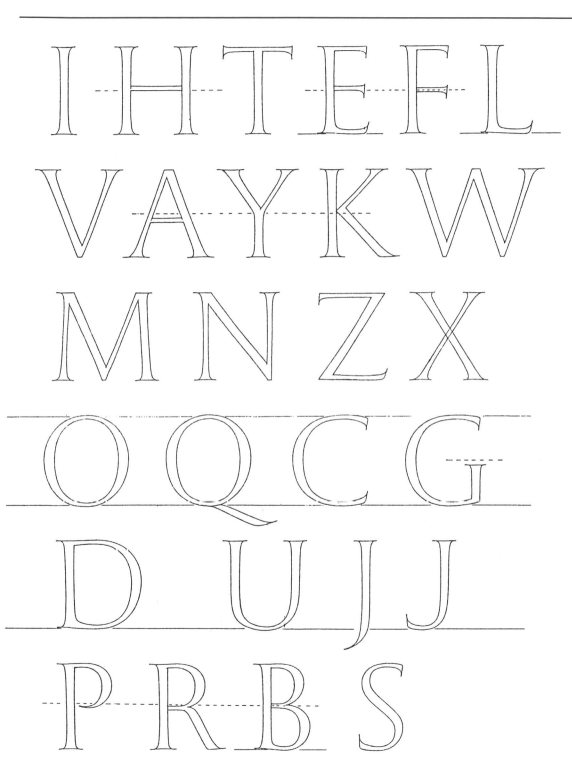

Versals

Versals were used in early manuscripts to mark verses, paragraphs and chapters. Frequently in the margin, they added colour and adornment and greatly enriched both page and book. They are widely used by calligraphers today and exist in many versions.

Deriving from Roman capitals and "built up", they are characterised by a stronger contrast between the thick and thin strokes. Their vertical stems tend to be top-heavy, and their serifs, unlike the "Roman" which mould into the stem, are thin, hairline strokes. The "bulging" form with more sensuous curves is referred to as Lombardic.

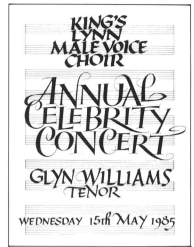

Concert programme using flourished versals.

ABCDEFG
HIJKLMN
OPQRST
UVWXYZ

Versals may be drawn with a pen about 1/3 the width of the vertical stem, which in turn gauges the thickness of the horizontal bar. They may also be drawn with a thin pen or pointed brush. Hairline strokes form clean serifs at right angles to the main strokes; large letters revealing a slight arc to these. Versals may be drawn with great freedom providing a good fundamental letter shape is retained. They lend themselves well to decoration, not only within the drawn shapes but outside as well.

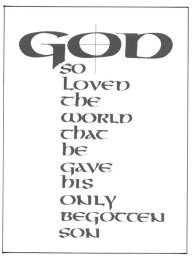

Uncials used on church service leaflet.

Uncials

Uncial writing was the standard book hand of scribes from the 5th to the 8th century and is to be seen in our oldest copies of the Bible. Very much a pen-made letter it is drawn with very little pen angle and frequently with the pen actually parallel to the line of writing. The flat-topped nature of the letters thus formed gives a pleasing emphasis to the "band-like" quality running across the page. There are alternative constructions for most of the letters and, depending on the subject, uncials should retain their essential, if specialised place in your repertoire.

ABCDEFGHIJ

KLMNOPQR

STUVWXYZ

ORGAN RECITAL

Gradual raising of right side of nib to form "trailing" strokes.

How to use Dry Transfer Lettering

Dry transfer lettering looks like printed type and works like most other transfers. It comes on thin plastic sheets each with a protective backing. It is transferred by rubbing the reverse side. Its capitals and lower-case letters are available in a great number of type faces, and many different sizes. Your local stockist can provide a catalogue from which you can select the most appropriate lettering for the type of work you are doing. Besides lettering, you will find other images – decorative borders, signs and symbols, tones, flags etc – which may be transferred to art work in the same way. It is more expensive to purchase large lettering because the sheet will contain fewer characters. Dry transfer lettering is useful for supplementary wording and will give a professional finish to posters. It also photocopies extremely well.

It is used very simply. Draw a pencil line on the art surface and remove the backing sheet. Position the lettering (or the spacing dots) on the guide line before lightly burnishing. Your stockist can supply you with a cheap plastic burnisher – a plastic knitting needle with not too sharp a point is one of many substitutes you can use. A final burnishing through the thin backing paper is advisable. Letters can be carefully scraped away with a sharp knife if errors are made. Spacing is an important aspect of dry transfer lettering. Visual spacing is the best method. Some advice on this is given in another part of the book.

Using dry transfer lettering.

Poster and programme design. White
transfer lettering on dark background of
photograph.

Menu cover showing creative use of dry
transfer lettering.

Drawing Letters on Squared Paper

I devised this alphabet so that the beginner might produce letters on squared paper. While not fully resolved it is useful for drawing very large letters by "scaling up". Note that the diagonals are drawn by outlining a strip of card which is the "down stroke" width. Top right of the illustration shows how easily "shadows" are introduced.

Programme cover. Freely drawn lettering combining with illustration.

Main Headings

The ability to draw strong letter shapes gives the poster designer fundamental advantages. Whatever is being advertised, the impact is better achieved by the use of bold lettering. Much practice will be required before you can work with confidence but here are a few points to help you achieve it.

1. Familiarise yourself with the lettering around you: shop fronts, bill-boards, TV titles, even paper bags, provide a multitude of helpful images.

2. Gather a scrap book of lettering styles to provide ideas and inspiration, and don't be afraid to trace letters from established alphabets.

3. Give your lettering "substance". There is nothing worse than "weedy" lettering overwhelmed by a vast "sea" of background. You can sometimes afford to break "x" height rules when you use wide pen or brush.

4. Recognise that the shapes between letters make an indirect but essential contribution to good design and appreciate the possibilities afforded by positive and negative shapes.

Part of poster which utilises music score as collage.

Poster for competition: brush with white poster colour on black sugar paper.

WORKING WITH A BRUSH & THE LARGER PEN

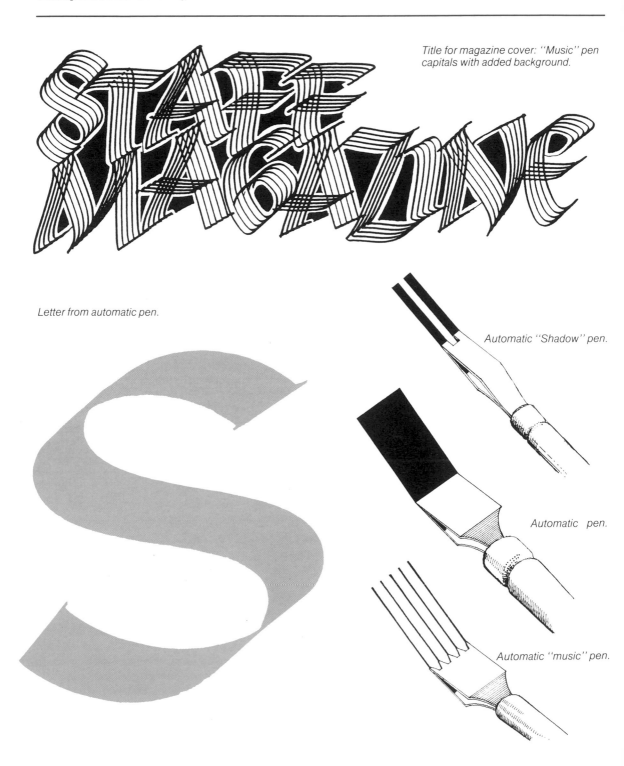

Title for magazine cover: "Music" pen capitals with added background.

Letter from automatic pen.

Automatic "Shadow" pen.

Automatic pen.

Automatic "music" pen.

Lettering from Osmiroid B6, B8 and
B10 poster pens.

Letter from "flat" brush.

Flat brush.

Water-colour brush.

STAFF ASSOCIATION

St. Valentine's
CHEESE & WINE
EVENING

Friday at 7 p.m.
14th FEBRUARY
in the College Hall

Tickets £5
obtainable from committee members

DESIGN AND LAYOUT

*Photocopied, reduced and hand-coloured
poster produced originally with Osmiroid
B3, B6, B8 and B10 pens.*

Suggested Procedure for a Formal Calligraphic Poster

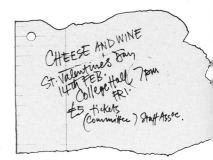

1. Check the details. It is not unusual to be left a scrap of paper similar to the one illustrated and there may be surprising omissions like the time or admission cost. Ascertain size and number of posters required.

2. Make rough sketches of possible arrangements. A symmetrical layout is a safe routine for beginners and it is this format we shall use here.

3. In producing lettering for the final rough, begin with the main heading. This, since it will feature the largest lettering, will establish the general proportion of the poster and govern all that is supplementary. Notice that I have allowed different sized capitals to "dance" between the guide lines, not only to give the words prominence but to create a less formal appearance overall. This and the additional information is now written on suitable paper and the units of information cut into strips.

4. On a piece of paper larger than your intended poster, lay the strips down "dry" to begin with. The method allows us considerable freedom at this stage, and the edges of the poster can be determined at the same time by adjusting strips of dark paper to simulate the exact borders. If you must adhere to a definite proportion, say for reduction to A4, the exercise might be more restrictive but the procedure will be all the more important.

5. When you are satisfied that all the lettering sits comfortably within its frame, stick down or tape the strips in position and mark the edges of your poster for subsequent trimming.

6. The hard work accomplished, you can now enjoy producing the final version of your poster.

Note: If your poster is to be photocopied or printed the "final rough" may be used as a master copy. Do remember, however, that the edges of paper strips are likely to leave shadow lines and should be "whited" over. Where reduction facilities are available your master copy is best produced proportionately larger (see "Scaling up"). Reduction reduces imperfections but take care that fine lines do not disappear completely. For reasons of economy and expediency it is likely that your poster will be produced in black and white but do entertain the idea of hand colouring small areas. They will add sparkle and enhance the most pedestrian design.

Preliminary roughs.

STAFF ASSOCIATION

St.Valentine's

CHEESE & WINE EVENING

Friday at 7 p.m.

14th FEBRUARY

in the College Hall

Tickets £5

obtainable from committee members

Too little margin.

STAFF ASSOCIATION

St.Valentine's

CHEESE & WINE EVENING

Friday at 7 p.m.

14th FEBRUARY

in the College Hall

Tickets £5

obtainable from committee members

Too much margin.

STAFF ASSOCIATION

St.Valentine's

CHEESE & WINE EVENING

Friday at 7 p.m.

14th FEBRUARY

in the College Hall

Tickets £5

obtainable from committee members

Correct margin.

B10 **CHEESE & WINE EVENING**

B6 **STAFF ASSOCIATION**

St.Valentine's B8 **Friday**

B8 **14th FEBRUARY**

Friday at 7 p.m.   in the College Hall

B8 **Tickets £5**

obtainable from committee members

Preliminary lettering.

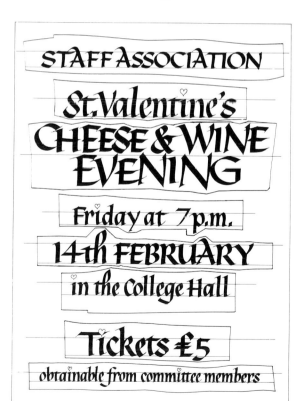

STAFF ASSOCIATION

St.Valentine's

CHEESE & WINE EVENING

Friday at 7 p.m.

14th FEBRUARY

in the College Hall

Tickets £5

obtainable from committee members

Organising layout.

The effect of bleach on dark ink (use only a nylon brush).

Lettering achieved by placing paper over incised lettering and rubbing with a wax crayon. If the ''rubbing'' is done with a white wax crayon or candle the subsequent application of water-based ink will produce a ''positive'' image.

Potato-print letters.

Writing with an air-brush.

Working in ink on wet paper.

USEFUL
TECHNIQUES

Collage

Using Collage for poster making has many advantages over more conventional methods and the results can be very striking. The materials required need not be expensive – indeed, the resourceful will hoard such things as magazines, scraps of fabric, used tickets, wrapping paper and unused wallpaper. Off-cuts from a local printer can also be useful. There are plenty of reliable adhesives around these days. Choose the most suitable – even cold water paste is adequate for newsprint and paper (don't worry about the mess, let the letters swim in it; it'll all dry out well in the end!) Spray adhesive is easy to use but a little expensive. Double sided tape and sticks of glue are handy. Self-adhesive coloured labels (almost too good to be true) are perfect for this "applied" technique.

Pushing letters and other shapes around is an excellent way of designing and collage workers soon come to recognise the importance of inter-related shapes. Aim for contrast – decorated letters on decorative backgrounds will be camouflaged and ineffective.

This is an enormously enjoyable activity and can be used both for the "one-off" job and for reproduction.

STUDENTS, MARY WARD COLLEGE

Collage poster made from newspapers and magazine letters, highly suiting the subject.

Easily changed collage arrangements.

Stencil and Spray

Anyone who has experienced the delight of pressing the button on the top of a can of Christmas silver spray and appreciated the accidental results caused by "masking" will realise the potential this activity holds in the field of poster-design.

As with collage, positive and negative shapes can be used, or combined, to create images which take into account the design qualities of background spaces. An airbrush is of course ideal, but the cheaper substitutes are most effective. Cans of paint spray are usually oil-based, so do shield areas that are not asking to be shrouded with paint, and consider working in a garage or shed!

The work illustrated here was produced with an inexpensive spray diffuser. Letters and masking materials should be cut from card. Thin card or paper will curl up when sprayed and has to be pinned down to obtain a sharp image. Heavier material like old brass letters and scrap such as vehicle gaskets are ideal, and many satisfying effects may be achieved when these shapes are removed, replaced by others, and additional spray applied.

Illustrations showing sequence and "build up" of spray, after movement of stencils.

Concert poster. Freely drawn lettering
and air-brush.

Correcting Errors

However careful you are and much as you may concentrate, mistakes are inevitable. If your work is of a very special nature, to be exhibited perhaps, then you will probably be better off starting again. But errors on "one-off" posters to be viewed from a distance, and art work for reproduction can be easily corrected. Opaque white and solutions used for blotting-out typing errors provide very swift results. When applied, they should be allowed to dry thoroughly before re-working. Alternatively, and in different circumstances, I find the following procedure very convenient.

Protect your desk or table with a piece of card and place an identical piece of paper to the one you are working on, underneath the area of the mistake. With a very sharp knife, cut with swift decisive strokes the area around your mistake to a depth that will also cut the paper beneath. Turn your art work upside-down and position the "clean" piece of paper in the space left by that bearing the mistake. Tape firmly into position. Finally, burnish along the joins with a round-headed plastic implement. The join on the correct side will be imperceptible but for photocopying purposes will require a touch of opaque white.

Resist Techniques

Quite a number of interesting and effective ways of lettering involve the use of "resist". Just as hot wax drawn on fabric protects the material from coloured dyes in the process of batik, so can letters (and other work) be similarly protected. The method simply relies on the inability of two materials to mix. Hence the writing done with a wax crayon or oil pastel will not accept the water colour which is brushed across its surface. Masking fluid, a rubbery solution, protects the surface very well and leaves very clean edges when it is removed with finger or eraser. It can be used in a "dip" pen (which should be cleaned frequently) but will spoil a brush so use an old one or a stick of balsa wood. The technique may also employ white poster colour as a protecting medium against water-proof inks. These and other coloured transparent inks produce very attractive results when they are built up one on top of the other.

"Resist" employing the use of white poster-colour and water-proof inks. The technique relies on the fact that while water will wash away poster-colour, it will not remove water-proof ink.

On a piece of strong cartridge paper the letter "A" has been painted in white poster colour. The surrounding area has been painted with green water-proof ink. The letter "A" has been washed away in running water and when the paper had dried white poster-paint was used to paint the letter "R". Turquoise water-proof ink was then painted in an area around it.

The painted "R" has been washed away, the paper allowed to dry and a final letter "T", protected with poster colour has been surrounded by carmine water-proof ink. A final wash reveals the full effect.

Masking fluid and water-colour.

Masking fluid and ink.

Wax crayon and water-based ink.

Using Photographs

If ever there was a cheeky way of making a poster then it's by using a photograph. It's fun looking for an appropriate picture, the mood of which can be serious, humorous or even eccentric. The unexpected can be stunning in its eye-catching qualities, and the idea is suitable for one-off notices and photo-copying alike.

PHOTOGRAPH BY MICHAEL HARRIS

Protest march photograph used to "fit the bill"!

Poster designed from "deliberately taken" photograph in local school.

Scaling

Rough sketches have a habit of looking far more lively than the enlarged version unless the process of "scaling" has taken place. The term is given to the enlargement or reduction of a piece of artwork and by doing this the essentials of proportion and composition are maintained. An enlargement is made by extending the diagonal of a picture. At any point along this diagonal a line drawn at right-angles to the bottom line will give you a new picture size. By "squaring off" both pictures the marks within a small square of the small picture can be easily transferred to the corresponding square of the larger picture.

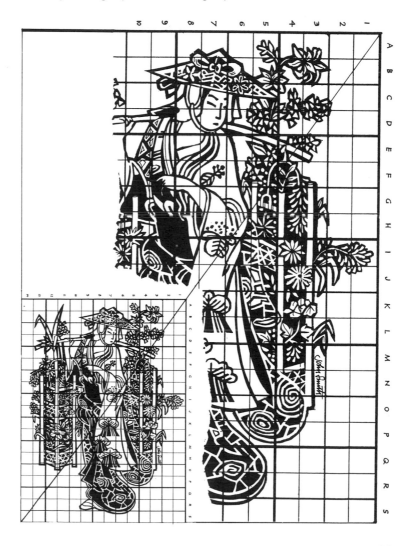

Making a Paper Print Poster

Here is the simplest of "relief" print-making techniques which will enable you to produce eye-catching posters with some easily obtainable materials. Not dissimilar to collage in application, the process goes a stage further when the surface of the work is "inked" with a roller and a print taken by burnishing the back of paper placed upon it.

Procedure

1. Produce a rough sketch as a guide.

Designing begins with a rough sketch.

2. On a piece of card, freely build up your design with paper shapes. Self-adhesive labels are very convenient (if glue is used make sure that the paper is stuck down well). Don't attempt to "draw;" think in terms of shapes and inter-related shapes. Don't be too conventional with the lettering and don't forget to work in reverse.

3. On a piece of plate glass, plastic, or hardboard, squeeze out a little oil-printing ink, flatten with a palette knife, and roll with a roller.

4. "Ink up" your relief block with the roller, transferring ink from the slab to the prepared surface.

5. Place a clean piece of paper over the relief block and burnish. The back of a spoon or a bone folder serves this purpose well.

Card with paper relief design.

Note: You may build up your relief block with such materials as textured paper, lace or net, even real leaves could have been used on the block which printed the poster featured. Print in coloured ink or on coloured paper; there are many combinations to experiment with.

Block partially rolled up with printing ink.

Removing the paper after burnishing.

The same block printed in black onto
paper which had been rolled with "ad
lib" colour.

Osmiroid Creative Leisure Series

Each title in the Osmiroid Creative Leisure series has been written in a lively "to the point" style, with very practical advice to ensure that exciting creative results are quickly achievable.

Chinese Brush Painting includes Chinese Calligraphy and a host of ideas from animal and plant subjects to landscapes.

Colour Calligraphy explains colour theory and shows some of the many ways that imaginative colour calligraphy can be created.

Pen and Ink Drawing leads the reader through many subjects and styles and includes enough "tricks of the trade" to ensure that everyone can create something.

The Art of Sketching shows the reader how to approach sketching from a very practical viewpoint, covering a wide range of indoor and outdoor subjects.

The Art of Stencilling gives the reader all they need to know to stencil onto walls, fabrics, furniture or paper, with manufactured or home made stencils.

Design and artwork by Nigel Long, Winchester

Printed in Spain